Extreme Freestyle Motocross Moves

By A. R. Schaefer

Consultant:
Jason Huggler
Promotion Manager
International Freestyle
Motocross Association

CAPSTONE
HIGH-INTEREST
BOOKS

an imprint of Capstone Press
Mankato, Minnesota

Capstone High-Interest Books are published by Capstone Press
151 Good Counsel Drive, P.O. Box 669, Mankato, Minnesota 56002
http://www.capstone-press.com

Library of Congress Cataloging-in-Publication Data
Schaefer, A. R. (Adam Richard), 1976–
    Extreme freestyle motocross moves / by Adam Schaefer.
        p. cm.—(Behind the moves)
    Includes bibliographical references and index.
    Contents: Extreme freestyle motocross—Basic tricks—Extreme tricks—Safety.
    ISBN 0-7368-1512-0 (hardcover)
    1. Motocross—Juvenile literature. 2. Extreme sports—Juvenile literature.
[1. Motocross. 2. Extreme sports.] I. Title. II. Series.
GV1060.12 .S43 2003
796.7'56—dc21   2002010762

Summary: Discusses the sport of freestyle motocross, including the moves involved
in the sport.

Editorial Credits
Angela Kaelberer, editor; Karen Risch, product planning editor; Kia Adams,
    series designer; Gene Bentdahl, book designer; Molly Nei, book designer;
    Jo Miller, photo researcher

Photo Credits
AP/Wide World Photos/Delly Carr, 20
Corbis/Duomo, 4 (top), 13 (top); Mark Jenkinson, 10 (top)
Getty Images/Al Bello, cover, 13 (bottom), 15; Darren England, 7, 18 (top),
    22 (top), 25; David Leeds, 8; Gary Newkirk, 12; Chris McGrath, 22 (bottom)
Raymond Gundy, 14, 24
SportsChrome-USA/Rob Tringali Jr., 4 (inset), 10 (inset), 16 (both), 18 (inset),
    21, 26 (both), 29

1 2 3 4 5 6 08 07 06 05 04 03

Table of Contents

Learn about:

- **Motocross basics**

- **Freestyle motocross history**

- **Competitions**

4

Chapter One

Extreme Freestyle Motocross

On June 29, 1999, extreme sports fans gathered near a dirt motocross course at the X Games in San Francisco, California. The fans were there to watch a new event called freestyle motocross.

At 15, Travis Pastrana was the youngest rider in the event. Pastrana revved his bike's engine as he started his first run. He completed trick after trick with no mistakes. He did a giant Superman, a lazy boy, and a heel clicker. He also jumped more than 29 feet (9 meters) in the air during a one-handed seat grab.

After Pastrana's ride was over, the judges showed their scores. Pastrana's total score was 99.0. Other riders tried to match his score, but no one could.

Pastrana then prepared to take his second run. He knew he was going to win and wanted to end the ride with something extreme. Pastrana jumped over a dirt ramp near the end of the course. He and his bike sailed more than 100 feet (30 meters) into the water of the San Francisco Bay.

The crowd stood and cheered. Pastrana had won the first X Games gold medal in freestyle motocross.

Motocross Basics

Motocross dirtbikes are similar to standard motorcycles. But motocross bikes are designed to drive over dirt or mud instead of paved roads or racetracks.

Motocross racing started in Europe in the 1920s. In North America, people started racing motocross in the 1940s and 1950s.

Freestyle Motocross

Freestyle motocross began in the mid-1990s. Some motocross racers began doing tricks after they fell behind during a race. These riders knew they had no chance of winning, so they did tricks to entertain the fans.

Most of the first motocross tricks came from bicycle motocross (BMX) riders. Later, motocross riders invented their own tricks.

Freestyle motocross began in the 1990s.

7

Freestyle motocross is part of the X Games.

Competitions

By 1996, racers held contests to see who could do the best tricks. In 1998, the first large freestyle event took place in Las Vegas, Nevada. Riders combined jumps with tricks on a dirt course. A team of judges gave the riders scores based on the number, difficulty, and performance of their tricks.

The International Freestyle Motocross Association (IFMA) formed in 1998. This group runs the largest freestyle series in North America. The IFMA hosts more than 35 events each year. Freestyle motocross events also are part of the X Games and the Gravity Games.

Riders lift their feet to do a no-footer.

Learn about:

- **One-handers and footers**
- **Whips and grabs**
- **Can-cans and heel clickers**

Chapter Two

Basic Tricks

Most freestyle motocross tricks are based on several moves. The first freestyle moves were simple, since riders were racing and performing tricks at the same time.

Hand and Foot Moves

Riders use their hands to perform some tricks. To perform a one-hander, the rider takes one hand off the handlebars. If the rider takes both hands off the bars, the move is called a no-hander. Some riders take both hands off the bars just before landing a jump. This trick is called a no-handed lander.

Riders twist the back of the bike during a whip.

Riders perform similar tricks with their feet. If riders lift one foot off a footpeg, the trick is called a one-footer. If they take both feet off the footpegs, it is called a no-footer. If riders lift both their hands and feet, the trick is called a nothing.

Whips

The whip was one of the first freestyle tricks. To do a whip, a rider twists the back of the bike so it is sideways in the air.

Riders can make this simple trick more difficult by increasing the force of the twist. The best riders can lay their bikes almost parallel to the ground during a whip.

Grabs

Riders perform different types of grabs. During a fender grab, the rider lets go of the handlebars and grabs the front fender. The rider's legs hang around the seat.

Riders also perform seat grabs. A Superman seat grab is more difficult than a fender grab. During a jump, a rider lets go of the handlebars and grabs the side of the seat. The rider's legs hang straight behind the bike. The rider looks like the comic book character Superman in flight. When a rider grabs the seat with one hand, the trick is called a one-handed Superman seat grab.

A nothing.

A one-handed Superman seat grab is a difficult move.

Can-cans

The can-can is another basic trick. In a basic can-can, the rider moves one leg over the seat. Both legs are on the same side of the seat. One leg is on the footpeg and the other leg is stretched out from the bike.

Some riders do more difficult forms of the can-can, such as the no-footed can-can. In this move, the rider takes both feet off the footpegs. The rider flips one leg over the seat and then stretches out both legs.

Many riders perform no-footed can-cans.

14

The heel clicker is popular with motocross fans.

Heel Clickers and Rodeo Airs

The heel clicker is popular with motocross fans. To perform this trick, riders lift both feet above the handlebars. They then wrap their legs around their arms while keeping their hands on the handlebars. They finish the trick by clicking their heels together above the front fender.

A rodeo air is similar to a heel clicker. To do a rodeo air, a rider does a heel clicker while holding one arm in the air.

Extreme Freestyle Motocross Slang

bail—to jump off the bike before it crashes

brain bucket—helmet

chicken soup—a trick that does not go
as planned

dead sailor—a rider who does not do a trick
during a jump

dialed-in—a ride or trick that is going smoothly

gravity check—a crash

pinned—to ride with the bike's throttle
wide open

run—several tricks performed in a row

sick—great or good

During a rock solid, the rider appears to fly.

Learn about:

- **Rock solid and cliffhanger**

- **Heart attack and kiss of death**

- **Shoe box and striper**

Chapter Three

Extreme Tricks

Once motocross riders learn basic tricks, they move on to more difficult tricks. Some riders take a basic trick and change it to make it more difficult. Other riders invent their own tricks.

Difficult Tricks

A few riders can do a more difficult version of the Superman seat grab called the rock solid. The rider lets go of the seat while in the Superman position and stretches out both arms. No part of the rider's body touches the bike. The rider appears to be flying through the air for a few seconds. The rider then grabs the seat again and gets back on the bike.

19

Carey Hart invented the heart attack.

The cliffhanger is another difficult trick. To do this trick, riders jump off their bikes and catch the toes of their boots on the handlebars. At the same time, they raise their arms in the air.

Carey Hart and the Heart Attack

Riders have invented some tricks or made them famous. Carey Hart is known for a trick called the heart attack.

To perform a heart attack, the rider grabs the handlebars with one hand and the seat with another. The rider then lifts both legs into a handstand.

Riders' boots touch the handlebars during a cliffhanger.

The nine o'clock nac-nac is a form of the nac-nac.

The bike is vertical during the kiss of death.

Nac-nac and Kiss of Death

Jeremy McGrath invented one of the first freestyle tricks, the nac-nac. This trick is the opposite of a can-can. To do a nac-nac, a rider does a whip and swings one leg over the rear fender to the other side of the bike.

Some riders do other forms of the nac-nac. For a nine o'clock nac-nac, a rider swings both legs to the side. The rider then throws both legs in the air behind the bike.

Rider Mike Jones first performed the kiss of death. For this move, the rider throws the bike into a vertical position. The rider then does a handstand while holding the handlebars.

Ryan Leyba invented the shoe box.

Shoe Box and Striper

Ryan Leyba invented the shoe box. To do this trick, the rider stands straight up on the bike's airbox. This part of the bike is behind the seat.

Ronnie Renner invented the striper. During this trick, the rider stands on the front of the bike. The rider then bends back over the seat and kicks one leg in the air.

A rider bends back over the seat during a striper.

Safe riders always wear helmets.

Learn about:

- Training places
- Equipment and clothing
- Motocross groups

Safety

Freestyle motocross riders work to keep their sport as safe as possible. Still, even the best riders sometimes crash. Good safety equipment and practices are as important as a good bike.

Safe Places to Train

Freestyle riders practice their tricks until they can do them well. Some riders practice at outdoor motocross tracks. These tracks are used often and have been tested for safety. Other riders practice on their own freestyle motocross courses.

Safe riders do not practice alone. Another person can call for help in case a rider crashes.

Safety Equipment

The motocross bike is one of the most important pieces of equipment. Safe riders check their bikes before each practice and competition.

Riders wear equipment to protect themselves. They wear helmets while training and during events. Riders wear goggles to protect their eyes from flying rocks and dirt. Some helmets have goggles built into them.

Clothing

Riders protect their skin from scrapes and bruises by wearing pants and long-sleeved shirts. The shirts are made of polyester. This lightweight material allows the skin to breathe.

Riders wear body armor under their shirts. This plastic shield has a layer of foam next to the rider's skin. Body armor protects riders during crashes.

Riders also protect their feet and hands. They wear leather boots with steel toes. Leather gloves both protect the hands and help riders grip the handlebars.

Motocross Groups

Motocross groups work to keep riders safe. The IFMA is one of the best known of these groups. Riders in IFMA events must wear safety equipment and follow safety rules.

Many freestyle riders also belong to local or national motorcycle clubs. The American Motorcyclist Association (AMA) is the largest motorcycle group in North America. The AMA works with riders and race organizers to keep riders safe.

Pants and long-sleeved shirts protect a rider's skin.

Words to Know

body armor (BOD-ee AR-mur)—a plastic shield with foam lining that motocross riders wear under their clothing

fender (FEN-dur)—a covering over a motorcycle wheel that protects the wheel from damage

freestyle (FREE-stile)—a motocross style that includes tricks and jumps

goggles (GOG-uhlz)—glasses that protect the eyes

polyester (pol-ee-ESS-tur)—a lightweight material often used to make clothing

To Learn More

Blomquist, Christopher. *Motocross in the X Games.* A Kid's Guide to the X Games. New York: PowerKids Press, 2003.

Maurer, Tracy Nelson. *Freestyle Moto-X.* Radsports Guides. Vero Beach, Fla.: Rourke, 2002.

Schaefer, A. R. *Motocross Cycles.* Wild Rides. Mankato, Minn.: Capstone Press, 2002.

Useful Addresses

American Motorcyclist Association
13515 Yarmouth Drive
Pickerington, OH 43147

Canadian Motorcycle Association
P.O. Box 448
Hamilton, ON L8L 1J4
Canada

International Freestyle Motocross Association
2501 Parkway Drive
Suite 105
Fort Worth, TX 76102

Internet Sites

Track down many sites about extreme freestyle motocross.
Visit the FACT HOUND at http://www.facthound.com

IT IS EASY! IT IS FUN!

1) Go to http://www.facthound.com
2) Type in: 0736815120
3) Click on "FETCH IT" and FACT HOUND will find several links hand-picked by our editors.

Relax and let our pal FACT HOUND do the research for you!

Index